ELISABETH

The Live and Legend of an European Saint

A Visual Voyage through Hungary, Germany,
Italy and Slovakia

ELISABETH

The Live and Legend of an European Saint

A Visual Voyage through Hungary, Germany,
Italy and Slovakia

Photography: Ulrich Kneise
Text: Jutta Krauß

Title *Holy Elisabeth by Tilman Riemenschneider,*
Teutonic National Museum Nuremberg, Franconia

2 *Memorial plate Hermann II, detail, St. George's Church Eisenach*

6 + 7 *Bükk Mountains, Hungary*

Bibliographic information published by Die Deutsche Bibliothek
Die Deutsche Bibliothek lists this publication in the
Deutschen Nationalbibliografie;
detailed bibliographic data is available in the internet: http://dnb.ddb.de

1st edition 2007
© 2007 Verlag Schnell & Steiner GmbH
Leibnizstraße 13, D-93055 Regensburg

Photography: Ulrich Kneise, www.ulrichkneise.de
Text: Jutta Krauß
English translation: Veronica Leary, info@bluestreak.de
Cover design, layout and typography: Denis Hopf, www.redtrump.de
Printing: Zanardi Group, Padua/Italy, www.zanardi.it

ISBN 978-3-7954-1996-7

For more information about the publisher's listings see:
www.schnell-und-steiner.de

Printed in Italy.

Index

Prologue

Her glance gives us the go-by, the holy Elisabeth. And yet we pause before this sublimely simple figure on the cover, searching for a dialogue with her, trying to recapture from the fine lines of her face the echoing image of her name in our memory. In Riemenschneider's sculpture we do not encounter a true to life effigy. The hand of the subtle master artist created a woman completely at peace with herself, not wholly of this world, full of dignity and magic. In this image one has the feeling of recognizing Elisabeth, the very Elisabeth of whom one knows so many wonderful things, because her contemporaries described in detail her thoughts and deeds, bringing to light every dark, hidden corner of her life. They have handed down to posterity the picture of an altogether extraordinary personality. But don't we stand rather puzzled before this portrayal of a woman who, without a second thought, renounced all the worldly goods her birth and standing had blessed her with, in order to be at one with the lowest of the low in emulation of Christ, who forswore all privileges to perform good deeds at the bottom ranks of society? How should the message of her story, which is repeatedly spoken of, be translated into the language of our present day?

The, for Elisabeth, binding faith in God that could move mountains in order to overcome each and any obstacle, is for us, living in our thoroughly materialistic oriented world, almost suspicious. Weren't such characters simply conceived, embellished with every ideal attribute, and conventionalized as the epitome of human perfection, in order to teach meekness to the many who fate had treated more step-motherly and to, at least, warm their souls in an otherwise cold and heartless world?

Elisabeth was an authentic person. The places where she lived and her world have disappeared to a large degree; time has taken its toll and changed them beyond recognition. And although the fantasy of generations has weaved many fairytale and false charm threads into the fabric of the 800 year old portrait canvas of Saint Elisabeth, we can at least be sure that she must have, indeed, led an extraordinary life. The world has time and again brought forth larger than life personages, such as the young princess, with enough power and courage to spring the bounds of the prevailing norms. They were completely misunderstood by their peers and everyone else and, rather than being honoured, they were regarded as being deranged. And in the actual sense of the word that is what they were: *desreng* = not in rank/line with the rest of the world because they viewed things from a different, higher perspective. Elisabeth lived a life of deeply felt humanity in keeping with the ideals of early Christianity. Her memory will thus survive the shifting tides of time and history.

This volume constitutes a further, but perhaps somewhat different addition, to the countless books about Thuringia's holy woman. It aims, above all, to bridge the gap of time and space using pictures. It makes allowance for the misty murkiness adhering to the distant

Middle Ages, despite all of our acquired and extended knowledge. It respects the ultimately mysterious component of mortal beings which evades even the cleverest analysis. And it surrenders itself to the wonders of the world – be they legendary memories, testimonies which have survived and been handed down to us from the distant past, the artistic creations of pious devotion, or the loveliness of timeless nature. Beyond the brief texts and picture panorama on its pages, this book would like to call forth associations to encourage readers in their own attempts to emulate Elisabeth's spirit. Her biography seems to be made up of legends and, as a life really lived, is very strange, but it constitutes, nonetheless, an inner cohesion of humankind.

12 + 13 Basel tapestry, Wartburg, Thuringia

13

14 *Hellgrevenhof, Eisenach, Thuringia*

15 *City fortifications, Sárospatak, Hungary*

KLINGSOR

VIDEO STELLAM LVCENTEM SVPRA H VNGARIAM

The "Holy" Heritage of the Hungarian

No one knows exactly on which day Elisabeth was born, nor where her cradle actually stood. When July 7th 1207 is presupposed to be the date of her birth, this is only due to the fact that it is the earliest possible date that can be calculated on the basis of her older brother Bela's documented birth date. Her parents, King Andreas II of Hungry and his spouse Gertrud, wandered with their royal entourage throughout the land, as was usual during the Middle Ages, holding court at various castles and towns open to them.
Among them, the Eastern Hungarian Sárospatak has been viewed since the 15th century as Elisabeth's most likely birthplace. Nowadays, only some remnants of the former royal palatinate which once bordered the banks of the Bodrog River can be found in Sárospatak with its mighty Renaissance castle. The landscape along the river vanishes into the vastness of the Puszta, but on the northern horizon the blue chain of the Bükk Mountains can be seen. If Elisabeth, as a child, had ever really seen these views, it is rather improbable that she would have been able to recall them later to memory. For the girl, sent to a foreign country at an early age, any memory of Hungry's actual landscape must have faded, giving way to an etherealized longing for home painted as a wonderland
And yet the Hungarian Empire was no less than that, and the bosom of the family anything but an idyllic refuge of warmth and security. Overshadowed by quarrels lasting for years with his own brother, King Emerich, Elisabeth's father Andreas married Ger-

trud from the Southern German lineage of Andechs-Meran earls, sometime after 1200. While Andreas himself was held prisoner, his brother sent the young bride, his sister-in-law, back home, a fate which almost repeated itself with her daughter Elisabeth. After Emerich's death, Andreas had no scruples about getting rid of the young heir to the throne, still a child. In 1204 he and the returned Gertrud received the crown and sceptre of Hungry. At this point in time, the royal dynasty of the Árpáds was able to look back on three hundred years in power, but in a ruling house mistrust stands ever on guard at the door. The Magyars, renowned for their unbridled temper, often forced Andreas to concede crippling concessions and revenged themselves on the queen after she had showered her German countrymen with offices and privileges. Described as power hungry, Gertrud was slayed in 1213 without mercy. Elisabeth's holy heritage? Sanctity is not exclusively precluded by a life of self-denial and remorsefulness in the evangelical sense of the word, but political diplomacy and ecclesiastical pragmatism also play their part, allowing many a worldly conqueror and despot to be quickly crowned and canonized. The nimbus applied to both the Árpáds, as well as the Andechs-Merans. Hungry, bulwark against the heathen tribes of the East and a borderland to the Byzantine Empire and orthodox Christianity, played a key and volatile strategic role for all parties concerned. Without giving up their long-standing friendly relationships with Constantinople, also characterized, of course, to a certain degree by hopeful covetousness, Hungarian rulers, from the 10th century on, oriented themselves more and more towards the West and the Church of Rome. Stephan I received the royal crown in the year 1000 with the blessing of the Pope. Thanks to the zeal from their own ranks, he and two of his descendants were canonized.

The Andechs family was descended from Saint Hedwig from Silesia, the patron saint of Berlin, among other things. Of Elisabeth's other aunts and uncles, mention can be made of Mechthild, an abbess in Kitzingen, Bishop Ekbert from Bamberg and Berthold, the patriarch of Aquileja and the second highest ranking prelate after the pope. It doesn't make sense in connection with Elisabeth, however, to speak about a family propensity towards religiousness, in particular since she grew up afar from her relatives and could have known of her saintly ancestors only through stories told to her. Although the fear of God and faith permeated profane life in the Middle Ages to a much deeper degree than we can imagine nowadays, neither the former nor the latter approach provide the essential clue for solving the mystery of Elisabeth's life.

20 + 21 Castle Rákóczi on the River Bodrog, Sárospatak, Hungary

22 Remains of the Romanesque round church, Sárospatak, Hungary

23 St. Elisabeth's Church, Sárospatak, Hungary

24 + 25 Lowlands along the Bodrog, Tokay region, Hungary

26 Arrival at the court, fresco detail, Wartburg, Thuringia

27 Church of Bodrogolaszi near Sárospatak, Hungary

LANDGRAVIATE THURINGIA

Did the King of Hungry promise his daughter to the scion of a provincial careerist? No. Although just a pawn in the political power play of her elders, the four-year-old princess was sent to the extremely splendid court of one of the most important German princes of the realm, In comparison to the Árpáds, though, the Ludowings were political high-fliers.

It took less than a century for the Mainfränkisch family of counts to go from laying claim to nothing more than the now long-lost castle of Schauenburg to achieving a position of hegemony in Thuringia. Ludwig der Springer's memorial slab, which can be found today in the St. George's Church in Eisenach, gives him grave, determined features. He is depicted with his right hand lying on his coat of arms and, with his left he is handing over a model of the Reinhardsbrunn Monastery under the patronage of the Ludowing family. Founder of the Wartburg in 1067, this Ludwig had no intention of remaining just one among a host of other counts. According to the saga, at least, this is the exact date given for the foundation and it might be quite right, since the castle is mentioned in Bruno von Merseburg's chronicle "Sachsenkrieg" in 1080.

Ensconced behind the exclamation "Wart Berg, du sollst meine Burg tragen" (Wait mountain, you shall carry my castle) which Ludwig is quoted as saying, is the successful occupation of alien territory. Shortly there afterwards towards the east, the stones of Neuenburg Castle started to tower above the Saale River. Not particularly

squeamish in his choice of methods for achieving power and, conse-
quently, plagued in old age by remorse, the enterprising count
founded the monastery at Reinhardsbrunn. He transferred the proper-
ty title for Schauenburg Castle to the monastery and in advanced
old age entered the monastery himself, safe in the knowledge that
his descendants would carry on the expansion he had initiated.
And, indeed, they did. In around 1130 the Emperor Lothar II rewarded
his Ludowing partisan with the title of landgrave, a few years later
the family came into the possession of large parts of Hessen due to
a propitious marriage, and, after Ludwig II had married the Staufer
Jutta, he found himself in the role of brother-in-law to the German
emperor at the crowning of Friedrich I Barbarossa in 1155.
The Great Hall of Wartburg, built between 1156 and 1172, thus gives
one inevitably the impression of being a symbol of triumph, lord-
ing it proudly over the land. The massive edifice reveals the musical
aesthetics of its arcades and the variety of motifs in the capitals,
once counting 200 in total, only on closer inspection.
Does the building's architecture divulge the aesthetics of its owner?
While still always keeping a sharp eye on political developments,
the Thuringia landgraves, from at least the turn of the 12th century
on, were also very interested in culture. Under Hermann I, ruler
since 1190, a taste for literature developed and the greatest poets
of the time were welcomed at the court of the landgrave. Heinrich von Veldeke, travelling from Lorraine, completed his "Eneit"

at Hermann's commission. Walther von der Vogelweide praised Hermann's open hand and described rollicking festivities, Wolfram von Eschenbach enjoyed Hermann's prolonged hospitality and wrote his novels at his castle. When the writer on occasion would hold up a mirror for the artistically minded landgrave to have a critical look at himself, he did it a manner that the shady sides of Hermann's political machinations could fade subtly into the background. The landgrave, always on the lookout for his supposed advantage, served first the one, then the other contender in the bitter conflict between the Welf and Staufer dynasties for control over the imperial crown; all to no avail. The battlefields shifted from place to place in Thuringia, leaving ever in their wake scorched earth. This fabulous friend of the arts, but also unscrupulous tactician for whose salvation his pious wife Sophie prayed so ardently, was hardly well loved. Through the contrivance of a cleverly arranged marriage and the arrival of the Hungarian king's daughter Elisabeth in Thuringia, his court achieved a position in posterity that it would hardly have gained on its own merits.

32 *Schauenburg Castle, Friedrichroda, Thuringia*

33 *Ludwig der Springer, Eisenach, Thuringia*

33

40 + 41 *Eckartsburg Castle, Eckartsberga, Thuringia*

42 + 43 *Reinhardsbrunn Monastery, Friedrichroda, Thuringia*

44 + 45 *Creuzburg Castle over the Werra, Creuzburg, Thuringia*

THE EXOTIC ROYAL CHILD

Right after the arrival of the four-year-old Elisabeth at the landgraviate court, so the chronicle reports, the little child bride was laid in a bed with her betrothed, a boy bridegroom – a poignant picture that blinds out the real background behind the Thuringia-Hungarian marriage alliance. The alliance's mediators, Elisabeth's uncle Bishop Ekbert of Bamburg and his brother, both suspected and hounded for being accomplices in the murder of King Philipp II, fled to their sister Queen Gertrud in Hungry in 1208/09. While Ekbert spent almost two years in Hungry, the bitter struggle for the throne continued to rage in Germany between the Welf Emperor Otto IV and his Staufer rival Friedrich. The coalition of princes in favour of the Staufer candidate, on whose bandwagon Hermann had once again jumped, promised every chance of success and was looking for strong allies. In this situation, Hermann could best secure the favour of the Hungarian king and bring to bear his influence on the Andechs-Merans by bringing about an appropriate marriage contract. The proposal was accepted and immediately implemented.

As early as the autumn of 1211, the Thuringia envoys – led by Chevalier Walter von Vargula, a brother of the landgraviate steward – met the Hungarian princess and her entourage at Pressburg. The procession would presumably have arrived in Eisenach some weeks later. What went through the mind of the little Elisabeth during her journey through the Thuringia woods, what did she feel when she caught her first glimpse of Wartburg and was introduced into the circle of a strange new family? A companion of almost her same age by the name of Guda was sent along with Elisabeth. She presumably remained her closest intimate. Growing up among the children at the court of the landgrave, Elisabeth must have attracted attention at a very early stage. Laughter and a frolicsome temper would give way, without warning, to the deepest sense of gravity. The child would break off her play to kiss the church door or would run into the court chapel and fall on her knees to pray before the crucifixion of Christ. In the middle of the merriest round dances, she would suddenly stop and, "for the love of God", stand for a time transfixed in devotion. When Elisabeth gave presents to poorer playmates, which often happened, she would demand in return that they recite a Our Father or Ave Maria. Guda and Elisabeth's lady-in-waiting Isentrud both later reported on such strange incidences. Should one suspect that the two witnesses in Elisabeth's canonization hearing simply wanted to glorify her, or were they describing a particularly sensitive child that was trying to come to terms with deep and conflictive impressions?

At Hermann's castle crude violence stood in stark contrast to its sensibility for courtly aesthetics and spirituality. For a soul with an open eye and heart, the contradiction between the princely pomp of the castle and the human misery in the filthy lowlands of the towns just outside its walls must have been crass. The spectre of death, omnipresent there, also directly intervened in the life of the child. When she was just six years old, Elisabeth learned about the sudden demise of her mother. Three years later Hermann, presumably the oldest son of the landgrave, died unexpectedly, but no one knows whether he was Elisabeth's intended bridegroom or not. When the old landgrave, declining into dementia, also passed away in April 1217, one is supposed to have strepitously speculated about sending the strange king's daughter back to Hungry.

She had become an annoyance, suffering more from the perceptible rejection as the uncertain future. In this situation young Ludwig, who had become landgrave after the death of his father, stood up in Elisabeth's defence. Had she been promised to him from the start, or was it the case of his having learned to love the girl growing up next to him, so that he didn't want to live without her and defended her against hostilities?

Contemporary witnesses spoke of a love match when Ludwig and Elisabeth wed each other in 1221, which was highly unusual when it came to dynastic alliances that were, by and large, politically motivated.

50 *Castle of von Vargula, Großvargula, Thuringia*

51 *View towards the south west, Wartburg, Thuringia*

52 *Greeting, Elisabeth cycle, high altar Kosice, Slovakia*

53 *Wartburg, Thuringia*

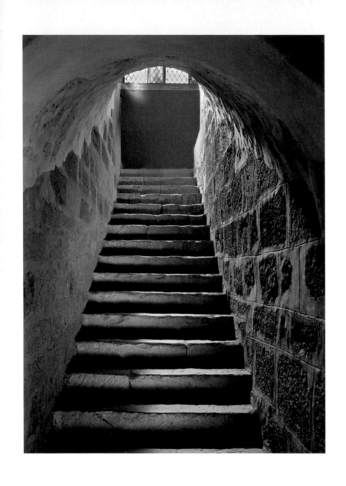

54 *Great Hall, Wartburg, Thuringia*

55 *John the Apostle, Eisenach,Thuringia*

56 + 57 *Double chapel of Neuenburg Castle,*
Freyburg, Saxony Anhalt

58 + 59 *Lower church of the double chapel,*
Neuenburg Castle Freyburg, Saxony Anhalt

Marriage Years

The picture of a richly dressed landgravine sitting at a distaff in view
of her playing son projects an idyllic image of a pastime of domes-
tic harmony. Spinning wool, though, was not a conventional activity
for a lady of her station, and this was even less so when the finished
yarn was destined for the Franciscan mendicants. Elisabeth increa-
singly saw her own self-defining goal in their ideal of living a Christ-
like life of poverty and mercy dedicated to God's word. Just as when
she was a child, the young princess did not conform to what was
considered appropriate for her station. Even her devoted ladies-
in-waiting grumbled when they were supposed to follow Elisabeth
into the stinking hovels of the town, loaded down with presents
to alleviate the distress there. The lady of the castle invited beggars
to dine at her table, she washed the feet of the poor, fed the weak,
even kissed the ulcerous wounds of the sick, and arranged for a
decent burial for the dead. Though giving away alms and providing
relief were considered the duties of the princely class, Elisabeth
transgressed every measure and limit. One must compensate for
extremes with extreme measures, she is supposed to have cheerfully claimed and to have shed tears of pity and joy as she went about
restlessly performing her good works. Could one embody states-
manship with such a sovereign princess and king's daughter, who
would stride to church dressed in a wool dress, sans jewellery and
crown, and sit herself among the poorest of the poor? Wouldn't
relatives interpret her actions as a provocation, those damned to

66 Elisabeth at the distaff, mosaic detail, Wartburg, Thuringia

poverty as a mockery of their misery? According to legend, her husband Ludwig sympathized with Elisabeth, he even praised her generosity and discretion in opening up the state granaries all over the land and distributing their stores during the hunger year of 1226. He must have supported his wife in the building of her hospital at the foot of Wartburg in which she administered to the most wretched of the sick. He didn't take any steps to stop her from lecturing magnificently costumed noble ladies for their haughtiness and demanding that they act more humbly.

One day, according to legend, Elisabeth was hurrying from Wartburg down into the town to bring some bread to the poor. She hid the bread in her cloak, though, because her husband didn't like to see her doing this. When Ludwig suddenly blocked her path and asked her what she was carrying, Elisabeth opened her cloak and the bread had been changed into roses.

Reality wouldn't have required any such wonder. As her ladies-in-waiting testified time and again, Elisabeth and Ludwig loved each other in a wonderful way, supported each other to the glory of God and corroborated together in his service. In her report Isentrud von Hörselgau differentiated between the necessary, worldly duties of the landgrave and the Christian missions of mercy by his wife. Prayer and benevolence were by no means, though, the only obligations of a pious sovereign princess. After just a year of marriage, Elisabeth gave birth at Creuzburg Castle to the hoped for successor to the throne, Hermann, who was followed by his sisters Sophie in the year 1224 and Gertrud in the year 1227. An affectionate and loving mother and wife, the very young wife also had the power of the keys over a considerably large court and her husband placed the regency of his realm trustfully in her hands during his frequent absences.

Though the twenty-year-old is also described as very competent and take-charge, she always felt bound by the exhortation of Jesus to act from the goodness of your heart in all one's dealings with the destitute, downtrodden and distressed. With the help of their confessor Konrad von Marburg, Ludwig and Elisabeth tried to resolve the conflict between the intimacy of a happy marriage, the worldly claims associated with their position and her zealous consciousness of being called to a mission. It was really only after the death of Ludwig that Elisabeth was able to resolve this dilemma.

70 *Knights' Hall, Wartburg, Thuringia*

71 *Elisabeth by Tilman Riemenschneider, Municipal Church Münnerstadt, Franconia*

72 *"Suffering Christ", fragment, Wartburg, Thuringia*

73 *Elisabeth, terracotta, Wartburg, Thuringia*

74 + 75 *Pest House, remains near Wartburg, Thuringia*

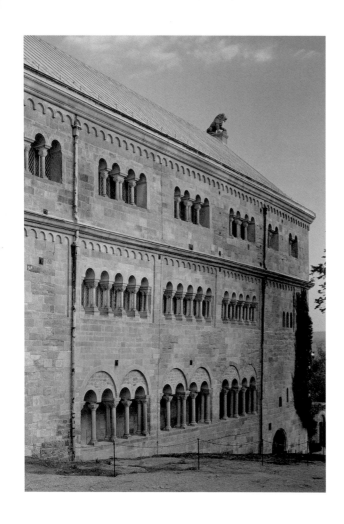

76 *West facade of the Great Hall, Wartburg, Thuringia*

77 *Gobelin, Museum Sacro Convento in Assisi, Italy*

78 Legend of the "Wonder of the Cross", altar cycle, Bardejov, Solvakia

79 Elisabeth's Bower, Wartburg, Thuringia

80–83 *Werra Bridge and Creuzburg Castle, Creuzburg, Thuringia*

84 *Birth scene, altar cycle, Bardejov, Slovakia*

85 *Lady's Bower, Creuzburg Castle, Thuringia*

86 + 87 Hospital scene, altar cycle, St. Elisabeth's Cathedral Kosice, Slovakia

88 Elisabeth visits the sick, painted glass, St. Elisabeth's Church Marburg, Hessen

89 Statue of Elisabeth, high altar, St. Elisabeth's Cathedral Kosice, Slovakia

FORAYS ON THE SIDE OF LUDWIG IV

In his vicious struggle to achieve his aims for expansion, Ludwig was hardly the "holy man" that people proclaimed him to be after his death. The young ruler was distinguished by political shrewdness,diplomatic far-sightedness and an energetic will to expand his power and possessions. Very soon after coming into power, Ludwig made use of the usual force of arms and burned down villages of the archbishop of Mainz, leaving the farming population without a livelihood. With the wardship of his nephew Heinrich, the future margrave, the Ludowing was able to conjoin his own claims to power when he had homage rendered to him as sovereign in the marches of Meissen and Lausitz, or when he marched against Polish Lebus, located on the Oder River, in order to extend his sphere of influence towards the east.

His amelioration of Neuenburg Castle to act as a military base for his aggressive Eastern policy and his negotiations with the Emperor Friedrich indicate that he was not willing his relinquish his gains when his ward came of age. In the end the emperor indemnified Ludwig not only with the Meissen territories in the event of Heinrich's death, but also promised him the land of the Prussians on the far side of the imperial borders – that is, in as far as it could be conquered. When Jutta, Ludwig's half-sister and the mother of Heinrich "der Erlauchte", attempted to foil these plans, the landgrave did not abjure a family feud, but laid her lands to waste and occupied Leipzig. Nonetheless, Ludwig showed himself to be, by and large, a competent imperial prince and a loyal vassal of the Emperor Friedrich II. He had to demonstrate this status, for example, by having the impressive double chapel at Neuenburg Castle built, but also by hosting festivities and receptions. The son, however, did not share his father's interest in courtly literature.

Thuringia's famous Muses court closed its gates under Ludwig IV and instead of Hermann's worldly round dances, religious mystery plays were performed. Reminiscence of Elisabeth or an expression of Ludwig's especial piety?

His vow in 1224, obligating him to participate in Friedrich II's crusade, at this point in time largely lacked its former religious euphoria, but was more a matter of following the political diplomacy of the Staufer emperor. For his retinue to Palestine the landgrave negotiated a payment of 5,000 marks from Friedrich. The emperor convened the imperial diet in the spring of 1226 at Cremona to clarify this and other questions pertaining to the crusade. Ludwig IV spent four months in Italy, leaving him a year after his return to prepare and outfit himself and his cortège for their Christian passage at arms. On June 24th 1227 the landgrave decamped for the south, accompanied part of the way by Elisabeth who finally made her tearful farewell. The army crossed over the Brenner Pass, traversed Lombardy and Toscana, and arrived on August 16th at the port of Brindisi where they continued their journey by ship. Ludwig fell ill with a typhoid-like fever and died in the presence of the emperor, the patriarch of

Jerusalem and the bishop of Akkon on September 11 th in Otranto. Landgrave Ludwig IV, without a doubt, was a key figure in Elisabeth's life. Without his tolerance for her philosophy of life and protective love, a landgravine, as Elisabeth is depicted by legend, seems inconceivable. Crown and cross were wedded inseparably to one another for Ludwig.

94 *Westarcade, Wartburg, Thuringia*

95 *Ludwig IV, St. George's Church Eisenach, Thuringia*

96 Landgraviate brakteaten, Wartburg, Thuringia
97 View from Runneburg Castle, Weißensee, Thuringia
98 Donjon, Wartburg, Thuringia

99 *Church and gate „St. Nicholas", Eisenach, Thuringia*

100 *Miracle of the Roses, fresco detail, Wartburg, Thuringia*

101 *Farewell scene, altar cycle, Bardejov, Slovakia*

102 *Alpine Brenner Pass, Italy*

103 *Ludwig IV, detail Elisabeth shrine, Sárospatak, Hungary*

104 *Prophet from the portal, Cremona, Italy*

105 *Front of the cathedral, Cremona, Italy*

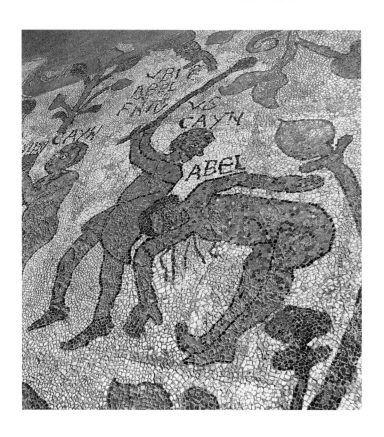

106 Fratricide, detail floor mosaic,
cathedral of Otranto, Italy

107 Staufer garrison, Lucera, Italy

108 + 109 "Crown of Apulia", Castel del Monte, Italy

110 *Emperor Friedrich II, Castel del Monte, Italy*
111 *"Staufer Pulpit", cathedral of Bitonto, Italy*

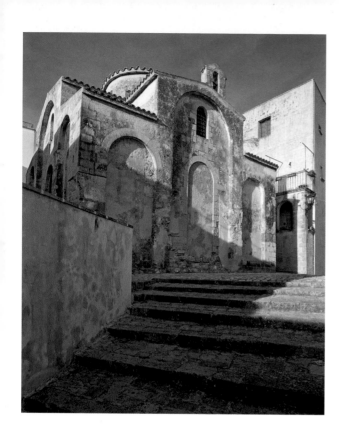

112 *Basilica of St. Peter's, Otranto, Italy*

113 *Olive grove with trollo, Otranto, Italy*

114 + 115 *Old town and harbor of Otranto, Italy*

A Preference for Poverty

To choose to be poor voluntarily seems absurd. From a pitying point of view, one generally regards poverty as an unintended burden, a lamentable deficiency, in today's materialistic society often enough as a failing. Going back to ancient times, it has been a commonplace tenet to regard the poor, counting among them also those who had to work for a living, as inferior, even as immoral creatures, without any consequence for society at large. Only wealth, or so one simple-mindedly reasoned, could free a person from any sort of existential constraints and allow one to live an honourable and laudable life. It is, therefore, no wonder that Jesus' gospel about the blessedness of the poor was regarded as indecent and as a dangerous and inflammatory profession. Even if Christianity had finally been tamed down and chained by the restrictions of the institution of the Church, it never completely lost its rebellious spirit. In the course of its history, time and again, voices rose in protest, calling for a return to the original principles of Christ, much to the consternation of the propagators of sanctioned doctrine. It would almost seem to be predestined that it was in 1207, the year of Elisabeth's birth, that the wealthy merchant's son Francis of Assisi renounced all his worldly goods in order to preach the gospel of God to the world as a barefoot beggar. The number of his disciples grew and in 1215 Francis achieved the papal acknowledgement of his order. As penitents and itinerant preachers, the Friar Minors spread his teachings beyond the borders of many countries.

Encountering the Franciscans in around 1224, the young Thuringia landgravine discovered an expression of her inner self in their sermons about the emancipating and glorifying force of living a life of poverty in keeping with the ideal of Christ. She requested the Franciscan lay brother Rodeger to instruct her in humbleness and patience in order to achieve exactly this goal.

Such a deeply felt and consequential belief in Christ elevated poverty to the status of a "lady", as Francis is literally quoted as saying. Typically, he called himself an "idiot" – a self-image that might appear to be grotesque but, from the judgement point of normalcy, was not that far removed. Neither Francis of Assisi nor Elisabeth of Thuringia were intellectually simple-minded fools. In their real lives, rather, they simply put into practice the Christian commandment to be as one with the lowest of the low, to love them and make them happy, to serve and be loyal to them, whereby social status and recognition did not play a role at all. The radical breach in St. Francis' life can only be understood as the complete identification with this ideal. This is also the only way to comprehend Elisabeth who, after Ludwig's death, also felt entrapped in a tangle of contradictory forces and, yet, made her way with uncompromising integrity.

It was due, not least of all, to the extremity of her example that Elisabeth shines out among the vari-formed mendicant movements of the 13th century which spread out all over Europe.

The growing bands of Friar Minors, beguines and Beghards were

the religious answer to the increasing social problems of the time.
It was a protest movement against the nobility, the rising educational
elite of the first universities and the traditional Church. In short,
it was a rebellion against the upper classes of society who neglected
their God given duty to see to the welfare of the poor and, instead,
indulged in vanity, avarice and corruption.
Aside from the needy sick, cripples, children and old people, and along
with the wars, bad harvests, famines and epidemic plagues which
continually contributed to the number of poor, the medieval concept
of poverty still also encompassed all those persons who had to work
for a living and, as from time immemorial, the irrelevant misery of
the deserted and forgotten.

120 + 121 *Assisi, Umbria, Italy*

122 *Porziuncola Chapel inside the Church of Santa Maria degli Angeli, Assisi, Italy*

123 *Francis, fresco detail, St. Francis' Church, Assisi, Italy*

124 *Hermitage Eremo delle Carceri, Assisi, Italy*

125 *Chapel of Eremo delle Carceri, Assisi, Italy*

126 *Saints Clara and Francis, fresco, Assisi, Italy*

127 *Franciscan Monastery San Damiano, Assisi, Italy*

128 + 129 *Last Day of Judgement, St. Kilian's Cathedral, Würzburg, Franconia*

From Darkness into Light

Elisabeth had just brought her third child into the world when the news of Ludwig's death was conveyed to her at the end of September 1227. For the young woman, it was as if a star had fallen from the sky and, what she could hardly have realized at this point in time, her whole world came crashing down with it. Faced now with open hostility from all sides of the family, her brother-in-law Heinrich Raspe went even one step further and detracted Elisabeth's widow's thirds which had been confirmed by documents. Since her confessor Konrad had issued her the commandment to only eat food from lawful sources, this meant that she was not able to consume any type of nourishment. It must have been on impulse and without planning things out, that the landgravine decided to turn her back on Wartburg. Accompanied by her loyal ladies-in-waiting Guda and Isentrud, she had the Friar Minors sing the Te Deum at midnight in the Franciscan chapel and spent the first night in a pigsty, happy to have made the break. Her situation became dangerous, however, when her children, who she had believed to be in safekeeping, were sent to live with her in her miserable living quarters. The little band of women and children suffered through the winter of 1227/28 in Eisenach under the most degrading circumstances, often begging in vain for help. A poor old woman who had once received alms from the hand of the landgravine, now maliciously pushed her benefactress into the mud of the lane. Elisabeth cheerfully picked herself up off the ground for the episode demonstrated that she finally didn't count as anything more than just another pauper among the poor. Her father, Andreas of Hungry and her maternal relatives, of course, attempted to provide swift aid, though to no avail. In the presence of Konrad von Marburg, Elisabeth took leave of her parents, her children, her own will and all worldly splendour on Good Friday 1228. Her son Hermann and daughter Sophie returned to the landgraviate court, while the six-month-old Gertrud needed her mother for a few more months. In the meantime, Elisabeth's uncle, Bishop Ekbert von Bamberg and her Aunt Mechthild, the abbess of Kitzingen, contemplated new marriage alliances in keeping with the young widow's station. Although Elisabeth vehemently resisted any such plans which collided with her vows, Ekbert detained her at the Franconian castle of Pottenstein till the beginning of April 1228. He didn't let her return to Thuringia until the conveyance of Ludwig's mortal remains and his funeral services took place.

Meantime, Konrad von Marburg, appointed as Elisabeth's ward by the pope, negotiated with Heinrich Raspe, not only for the payment of her widow's share of 2,000 silver marks, but also secured her the livelong usufruct of the landgraviate lands near Marburg. Konrad's success stood in opposition to Elisabeth's wish to live in Franciscan poverty, but it seemed unthinkable for him that the daughter of a king and a landgravine should descend to the level of a wandering beggar, the more so as he had promised to protect her. Even if he had seen his spiritual penitent as being called to a

higher sphere of influence, it would have been more usual, and certainly more in keeping with her station in life, for Elisabeth to have entered a convent. There would also have been no objection to such a step. This, however, she categorically rejected and is supposed to have asserted to Konrad: "I am going to do what you can't forbid me to do". The plan to found a new hospital gradually took shape in her mind as the means for allowing her to come closest to actualizing her aspirations unchecked. She wanted to live with Jesus Christ, but like him she wanted to make an impact on the world.
In the summer of 1228 she already began building a hospital outside the city of Marburg with her money, and whose community she was to join as an equal among equals.

134 + 135 *Warthurg from the north, Thuringia*

136 + 137 *Fragments, Runneburg Castle Weißensee, Thuringia*

138 *Heinrich Raspe, Eisenach, Thuringia*

139 *Wartburg Gate, Thuringia*

140 + 141 *Eisenach, Thuringia*

142 Humiliation, altar cycle, Bardejov, Slovakia
143 Flight from the court of the landgrave, Wartburg, Thuringia

144 *Cathedral from the north east, Bamberg, Franconia*
145 *In the Bamberg Cathedral, Franconia*

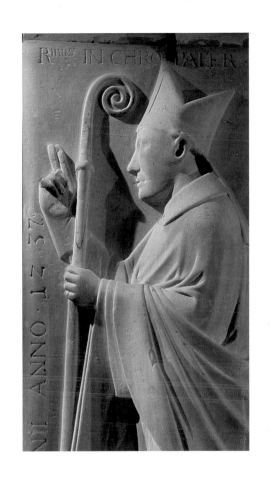

146 *Pottenstein Castle, Franconia*

147 *Bishop Ekbert, Bamberg Cathedral, Franconia*

Elisabeth's Hospital at Marburg

Elisabeth's establishment of the hospital in the western part of the landgraviate must have been to accommodate the Ludowings, since only Eisenach and Gotha had similar institutions. In keeping with the time and the purpose of the project, the facility was constructed of simple timber-framed houses and located just outside of Marburg's gates. Completed in the autumn of 1228, Elisabeth had the chapel dedicated to Francis of Assisi, who had just been canonized shortly previous to this time.

The first church north of the Alps with St. Francis as its patron saint became a place of pilgrimage with each pilgrim being promised 40 days of absolution. The chancel of the church opened into the adjacent infirmary, so that the patients who were confined to their beds could also participate as God's guest in the masses. The sumptuous blankets, sheets and pillows covering the sickbeds was commented on as late as 1235. The assets and dowry that her brother-in-law had conceded Elisabeth, she used for her good deeds. Giving away finery and clothes to the needy, she herself slipped on the plain grey garment of a religious woman. Her clothing wasn't the habit of any given order, but emphasized the vow of poverty made by one of the despised "sisters of the world".

Elisabeth had found her place in life. When she consigned the little Gertrud to the Premonstratensian convent at Altenberg, Elisabeth made a last, clear break, certainly not light-heartedly, with her former life. She also allowed Konrad to send away her companions

Guda and Isentrud. A very strict, serious-minded noble widow and a deaf virgin from the lower classes took their places, in order to increase Elisabeth's humbleness and patience, in keeping with his will. With his hard commandments, his canings for the slightest failure, Konrad's gloomy, ascetic figure must have overshadowed each and every act of disobedience in her young life. Since nothing would have been easier for the former princess than to have exchanged Konrad for a less stricter confessor, though, he must have, in all his inhuman stringency and boundless fanaticism, fulfilled Elisabeth's expectations; she needed help in leading a truly Christian life. Her avowed abnegation of any will of her own, however, cannot be taken at entirely at face value.

When Elisabeth really wanted to do something, she did it, and there are examples of when she defied the orders of her master.

He was very displeased when Elisabeth distributed the enormous sum of 500 silver marks to the poor on a single day. When she secretly, despite his forbiddance, bedded down and took care of a leprous woman in a remote corner, Konrad took up a whip, punished Elisabeth and hounded the woman away. It is documented that from early years on, Elisabeth addressed herself with particular devotion to lepers. For medieval people, leprosy was held to be a fate sent by God and a sign of his grace – it produced not only disgusting ulcers, but was also highly contagious.

What was the cause of her early death? Did her strength leave her,

as is generally assumed? Reports about Elisabeth predicting her imminent end, and her slow, gently smiling passing away, draw a strange picture which is reminiscent of medieval mystics.
She was cheerful and sang wonderfully on her deathbed. Elisabeth of Thuringia died peacefully in her sleep at the break of day on the morning of November 17th 1231, a little boy who she had once been able to cure, sat loyally at the side of her bed.
The body was laid out in the chapel of the hospital for two days to allow the people flocking in from all over to take their leave of her. The mourners were convinced that a saint had died. The first relics – hair, finger nails, scraps of her garment – already began to circulate within this short period of time. Hordes of the sick pilgrimaged to the little chapel, crowding around the plain tomb before the altar, and were miraculously cured.

152 *Tympanum, Hospital Church Ochsenfurt, Franconia*

153 *Elisabeth, relief in Kosice Cathedral, Slovakia*

154 St. Elisabeth's Church, Marburg, Hessen
155 Hospital scene, cathedral Kosice, Slovakia

156 Chapel, Hospital of the Teutonic Knights, Marburg, Hessen

157 Relief, Elisabeth Shrine, Marburg, Hessen

158 „The Holy Elisabeth and her Taskmaster
Conrad von Marburg", Philipps University
of Marburg, Hessen

159 Flagellation, detail from the tomb of the
Grand Master of the Teutonic Knights
Konrad, Marburg,

166 Statue of Elisabeth, Freyburg, Saxony Anhult

167 Exaltation of the bones, fresco, Wartburg, Thuringia

Epilogue

Jacobus de Voragine, the medieval Homer of the saints' legends, translated the name Elisabeth with "God's seventh one" in his Golden Legend, whereby the Hebrew name for God "Eli" is multiplied by "sabeth". The theologian and archbishop, born in Genoa shortly before Elisabeth's death, was thinking of the seventh day after the creation of the world, the Sabbath, which is the embodiment God's day of rest after he had finished his work and of the blessedness of God in all people. In the biblical number mysticism, seven stands for divine abundance, the eight for the resurrection and new beginning. Jacobus de Voragine placed Elisabeth between the two and, aside from the seven deeds of mercy, also assigned her seven statuses: those of a virgin, wife and widow, as well as those of an active doer, a person of reflection, a monastic ascetic and that of a glorified being.

In keeping with the first descriptions of her life and the recorded evidence of witnesses at her canonization hearing, a sacrosanct image as one of the "most modern" saints has developed, finding veneration in the whole world of Western Christianity.

Elisabeth's historically authentic biography can hardly be ascertained behind the conceit surrounding her person. Or did the spirited king's daughter who loved to pray ever really exist? Or the princess who chose to take on the tasks of the humblest servant?

The unnatural mother who deserted her children, the radical fundamentalist who lived in the inverse world of the gospel or the scandalous eccentric who had the courage to follow her calling from the very top to the very bottom of the social scale? Even if one suspects the loving memories of her closest companions, her ladies-in-waiting and servants, and her fellow nurses of the hospital at Marburg to be ethereal, and her spiritual guide Konrad to be ambitious for Elisabeth's canonization, one can hardly deny they were reporting about an altogether unusual woman, an anomaly.

She was venerated after her death by the world, her bones were bedded in a sarcophagus inlaid with precious stones, her head enclosed in a valuable vessel. One of the most splendid sepulchral churches of its kind was raised over Elisabeth's last resting place, the humble penitent of a transparent earthly existence.

It lay at the foot of the castle of the landgraves who now emblazoned themselves with saintliness of one of their family members. Musingly we stand before the monument in memory of the Hungarian saint of Thuringia, we envision the places where she was at home, places she knew, places people certainly told her about. In the far distance, we discover vestiges of her cognate essence. On this visual voyage, we seek to win new impressions, to establish eye contact. The geographical borders in which Elisabeth spent her life lose their importance, dissolving themselves into a timeless landscape of the sentient spirit.

171 *Elisabeth, painted glass, St. Elisabeth's Church Marburg, Hessen*

172 Elisabeth, fresco detail, St. Francis' Church, Assisi, Italy

173 Bakehouse and St. Elisabeth's Church Marburg, Hessen

174 + 175 *Place of canonization, San Domenico, Perugia, Italy*

176 *High altar, St. Elisabeth's Cathedral Kosice, Slovakia*

177 *St. Elisabeth's Cathedral, Kosice, Slovakia*

178 *Courtyard of St. Michael's Chapel, Marburg, Hessen*

179 *"Philippstein", Haina Monastery, Hessen*

180 *Feeding the Hungry, St. Liborius Chapel Creuzburg, Thuringia*

181 *St. Liborius Chapel of the Landgraviate Bridge, Creuzburg, Thuringia*

182 *The so-called "French Elisabeth", detail, Marburg, Hessen*

183 *Portrait of Elisabeth, Teutonic National Museum Nuremberg, Franconia*

Song of the Sun

" … Praise be to you, my Lord, by our Brother Wind and Air,
And the Clouds and all Weather,
According to your will, stormy or fair,
Through you that all things are guided.

Praise be to you, my Lord, by Sister Water,
How humbly useful she flows
How precious and pure are her joys.

Praise be to you, my Lord, by Brother fire
With which we chase away the darkness of night
Beautiful and friendly is his warming light.
Powerful and mighty his burning rage.

Praise be to you, my Lord, by our Sister, Mother Earth,
Who carries us gentle and strong,
Offering her fruits in many forms,
Bushes and herbs and flowers in bloom.

Praise be to you, my Lord, by those who for your love
Must suffer in patience trouble and pain,
Blessed are those who live not in vain. …"

Extract from "Song of the Sun" by Francis of Assisi (1181–1226)